A gift honoring Griffin and Carson Gilchrist

Ocean Life

Crab

By Lloyd G. Douglas

Welcome Books™

Children's Press®
A Division of Scholastic Inc.
New York / Toronto / London / Auckland / Sydney
Mexico City / New Delhi / Hong Kong
Danbury, Connecticut

Photo Credits: Cover, p. 11 © Royalty-Free/Corbis; p. 5 © Roger De La Harpe/Animals Animals; pp. 7, 19 © Photodisc/Getty Images; p. 9 © Richard I'Anson/Lonely Planet Images; p. 13 © Patti Murray/Animals Animals; p. 15 © Lynn D. Odell/Animals Animals; p. 17 © Farrell Grehan/Corbis; p. 21 © Annie Griffiths Belt/Corbis

Contributing Editor: Shira Laskin
Book Design: Elana Davidian

Library of Congress Cataloging-in-Publication Data

Douglas, Lloyd G.
    Crab / by Lloyd G. Douglas.
    p. cm. — (Ocean life)
    Includes index.
    ISBN 0-516-25027-2 (lib. bdg.) — ISBN 0-516-23740-3 (pbk.)
    1. Crabs—Juvenile literature. I. Title.

QL444.M33D68 2005
595.3'86—dc22

                                                      2004010109

1 2 3 4 5 6 7 8 9 10 R 14 13 12 11 10 09 08 07 06 05

Contents

Crabs are animals with hard **shells** on their bodies.

They are found all over the world.

5

Most crabs live in the water.

7

Some crabs live on land.

They live near the water.

9

Crabs have ten legs.

Their front two legs have **claws**.

Crabs use their claws to keep themselves safe from other animals.

13

Crabs also use their claws to eat.

Most crabs eat plants and small animals.

Crabs use their legs to walk.

They walk **sideways**.

There are many different kinds of crabs.

The largest crab is the Giant Spider Crab.

19

Many people like to eat crabs.

New Words

claws (**klawz**) the sharp, pointed ends of a crab's legs that open and close to grab things

crabs (**krabz**) animals with hard shells that live in or near the water

shells (**shehlz**) hard covers that protect living things

sideways (**side**-wayz) moving or directed toward one side

To Find Out More

Books
Crabs
by Jason Cooper
Rourke Publishing

Crabs
by Lola M. Schaefer
Scholastic Library Publishing

Web Site
Crab Enchanted Learning Software
http://www.enchantedlearning.com/subjects/Crab.shtml
Learn about crabs and print out a picture of a crab to color
on this Web site.

Index

About the Author

Lloyd G. Douglas writes children's books from his home near the Atlantic Ocean.

Content Consultant

Maria Casas, Marine Research Associate, Graduate School of Oceanography, University of Rhode Island

Reading Consultants

Kris Flynn, Coordinator, Small School District Literacy, The San Diego County Office of Education

Shelly Forys, Certified Reading Recovery Specialist, W.J. Zahnow Elementary School, Waterloo, IL

Paulette Mansell, Certified Reading Recovery Specialist, and Early Literacy Consultant, TX